AUGUST ZERO

OTHER BOOKS BY JANE MILLER

Working Time: Essays on Poetry, Culture, and Travel

American Odalisque

Black Holes, Black Stockings (with Olga Broumas)

The Greater Leisures

Many Junipers, Heartbeats

WESTERN STATES BOOK AWARD

AUGUST ZERO

JANE MILLER

COPPER CANYON PRESS

Poems in this collection have appeared in *American Poetry Review, American Voice, Black Warrior Review, Cream City Review, Denver Quarterly, Indiana Review, Ironwood, Kenyon Review, Ploughshares, Provincetown Arts, River Styx, Sonora Review, Volt,* and *Willow Springs.*

A broadside of "New Body," designed by Clint Colby and Charles Alexander, was printed by SUN/Gemini Press, Tucson.

A broadside of "Innocence" was printed by Karla Elling of Mummy Mountain Press, Tempe, Arizona.

In "The Poet," certain architectural details have been rephrased from *Re(Building)*, by Daniel Solomon, Princeton Architectural Press, 1992.

The author gratefully acknowledges the Lila Wallace-Reader's Digest Fund for a generous award which allowed her time to write this book.

Publication of this book is supported by a grant from the National Endowment for the Arts. Additional support to Copper Canyon Press has been provided by the Andrew W. Mellon Foundation, the Lila Wallace-Reader's Digest Fund, and the Washington State Arts Commission. Copper Canyon is in residence with Centrum at Fort Worden State Park.

The Western States Book Awards are a project of the Western States Arts Federation. The awards are supported by the Xerox Foundation, Crane Duplicating Services, and the Witter Bynner Foundation for Poetry. Additional funding is provided by the National Endowment for the Arts.

Jacqueline's Hayden's "Shore Birds in NYC" (Type-C print, 20 × 24″) is reproduced on the cover by permission of the artist.

Library of Congress Cataloging-in-Publication Data
Miller, Jane, 1949–
    August zero : poems / by Jane Miller.
        p.   cm.
    ISBN 1-55659-060-1 : — ISBN 1-55659-061-X (pbk.)
    I. Title.
PS3563.14116A93   1993
811'.54—dc20   93-4137

COPPER CANYON PRESS
Post Office Box 271, Port Townsend, Washington 98368

CONTENTS

FOR KIM

THE POET

You would procure the oil of forgiveness from the angel
at the doors, and get a small branch for a tree
that finds no use until it becomes a bridge over a river.
You have a premonition, while crossing,

about the wood's fate, and rather than step farther,
cross on foot. The wood lies dormant for centuries
until it's dug up and three victims die on it,
scattering the Jews. Unable to discern The
cross from those of two thieves, you place them in the pit
of the city and in the early hours hold each above

your head, and with the third are brought to life
zipping between buildings at high speed, shifting
into fifth out a disembodied ramp.
The thrill in the air is sexual, the ballpark darkened
and the holograph of the shut airport glowing,
your headlamps trained on mall light in fog made
more intimate and infinite by the collapse
of time, cement bits swirling your sealed space
to the strains of violins. It's the dawn of an era.

Time does not improve it. You live in a sunny place
and work in a sealed building. 10 mph on Interstate 405
by 2000. The twentieth century, begun in Vienna, has ended
in California.
. . . gas meters on your left and electric meters on your right.
Ahead, at the end of a passage, out in the light
a flight of concrete stairs. As you climb
you see the big towers of the financial district
fifty stories high a few blocks away . . .

The sense of entering a city nobly, walking the freeway at night

before it's torn down, hearing Portuguese, German, Japanese,
French, Chinese, seeing views of the bay, metallic, choppy,
and of the suspension bridge, and the ships, this is over.
About the demolition, a few warnings, like those about the earthquake.

The clack in the streets of Vienna, a carriage door slamming
and a continuous fountain, though far away, seem no farther
than the broken freeway. The bells of the tower, quiet.
The stones smooth and brilliant in moonlight.

You are in a car with music and air conditioning and a phone.
Softly, the classical station massages you.
You know in the back of your head
the best of your creative life has been siphoned away
by desire and money, desire in general and money in comparison
with others, but between one abstraction and another you yourself
quietly and fiercely participate in a disappearing place,
one you loved and were prepared to enter
with great humility, bathed in tears and barefoot.

ANY TWO WHEELS

Firecrackers thundering day and night, and lightning silences —

a few blossoms, the lowly mountains, that pair in the tunnel of love
                    — and it is a tunnel, and it is love —

it's almost like everyone is smiling on the streets of the government,
the weeds can touch us only so far up our legs
                    where it will be spring, spring when we get out —

easy to live without money, without equality and power
in a bar with a lemon fizz, dancing with the two or three best lookers,
a little older than one might have picked, hippier,

— no, it wasn't a holiday!
        — I only knew one such day in my life!
                — whose fault was it, as far as art was concerned?

the flower that very night I have in my hair, I shall talk about
                                            it briefly —
the end of the war did not bring liberty, and that seems to me
more dangerous than pain, my little anacin —

my arm ached from keeping that flower intact, I have quite a head
                                            of hair,
you see, and a blue poppy is hard to find, really is
a strain on the imagination, no?
— now when the firemen put out the stars I think of it, I

— it showed me how exhausted we had been, touching language
                                            directly,
and though nothing is conceivable for us now, the borders
of language fade — film, magnetic tape, mime — if you look closely,
down on one hand if need be, you'll see the discourse there,

incomplete, digressive,
the lovers kissing and arguing at the same time, the heat divine,
and as long as time permits, they go on smoking —
they think it's ok sleeping alone in space —
ascending and descending the misty grapes as if there is no art of
interruption
— and they are grapes, and it is misty —
now that everyone loves the taxman and embraces the police
whose lips are like berries too,
berries of course are now entirely terms, no amount of
gentility can conceal that fact but everyone is properly
instructed in sheer projection — listen,

a heart this big, if anyone's asking, utilizes
diamond chips, and in the poorest countries, as big as a ball of thread
which sticks to your hand and draws the boat ashore, where a hundred
years are as one day, that same woman weeping since the erection of a
round tower,
the first sign of official culture —
— was there a ridge with a lake on either side?
— beachfront and pink sand?

the sulphur sets and the sulphur rises like a minotaur,
our bodies are straight and perfect, daylight as black as a beetle,
and white as the snow of one night, all our nights.

AUGUST ZERO

Young trees the bright green of a moonless night,
lawn the red of scorpion, —

the pleasure dome drops, a drill ceases and a mower resumes.
It hides the spectacle of the mountains
and jolts us, it's been a long time
since we've had a little space to ourselves.

All the same, in spite of everything,
we are made to live in the air, which involves a certain number
of mental operations
the full force of a bow, a revision of the notion
of history,
oddly imitating the movements of animals when I think about it,
doubling back, appearing to be shot or struck —

and celestial sounds, not sound itself
rock the bare earth, packed hard·and nailed
to the tune of the unconscious,
which we regret to understand.

Don't get me wrong, there's still a knowledge of freedom,
a bath, a change of clothing,
possession of a child's heart,
a handshake, and the function of time
a detail — even in air
language is a
cross between an appetite and a mouth —

I'm not hungry when I'm lonely.
Like all the lead and neon which is forgotten
I forget that people have died forever,

no one knows you
and the ideal place is a dome with horses' shadows
the shade of steel gin,
and what formerly acceded to a view constitutes love.

A pear—
remember now future became present—
in a kitchen and two rooms in orbit
pins the horizon with its pony body and elk head
and we enact where we first made love the camellia of our beloved—
we can't touch exactly
but attempt a profound correlation—
we grip the skeleton of a river and the sun kisses it
like one's own throat.

This is the earth, my love, all of us
have a chunk on our backs.
You are an angel
and I am an ancient
who're cast from two and a half billion cars a day

into one copter night,
and closure is that windmill
through a wall in the circle, drifting
like the once innocent

oil spills in the Pacific,
like conversation.

SCATTERED ALPHABET

Our initial faith in the world, our father, if you will,
was not true enough —
everything we lack takes on definition and form.
For example, on a hunt for our parent sun,
a whole day, a whole city involved,
there's a sense of overdoing it, a monotone,
and when we find it, no longer yellow — never really —
looking at it, our headache is someone else's

      collapse in space. I cease weeping
in the mornings — mornings are now part of theater —
and when a planet roars by —
                honestly,
space is a world of play, there's no reason
why it shouldn't be — the continents wander like
huge rafts or lava-flows but without danger
of spilling since there's no down there's merely

five billion antecedents. There are substitutes
and assumptions where once there were summers
eating chicken and watermelon.
You are my brother when I write;
I kiss your face.

— when I see you I remember living with you,
      imitating you.

And when I try to dream another world,
a crystal of the continental crust — you can imagine the bondage
of those for whom description is redemption —
my soul dwarfs

          —I know the future
is included—
               that feverish afternoon
our brittle father and pretty mother
          marry again,
                    carbonate ooze to monsoon.

GIANTS

Someone's old parents in the desert on folding chairs,
one cradling his face, the other absorbed,

a Jew with blue eyes and a Jew with brown,
and inside, behind a huge plateglass window,

a modern dining area, black and white high-tech kitchen, swivel stools,
a lot of counter space,

and their daughter basting a turkey with orange sauce.
The father has only this morning

confessed his wife's secret — something he never tells her he knows,
though he assumes she knows

her father — who would be near 100 now — never died
when she was two, but abandoned his daughters and wife

and gave Florence and Rachel — lifted from the Bible — the gift
of the public trial of early sorrow,

which each wore far from her nature like a boxed jewel
that escapes down the throat and illumines the heart,

as the throbbing of the cosmos is lit
by what preceded it.

The man in the chair, whose leg won't work when he gets up,
has accepted his wife's anger as depression

and forgiven her, turning down the light
like an orchard lamp, low and steady, for fifty years.

I know them, I have bothered to inhabit every maneuver
until they shrivel and I am sky that darkens over

them — these creatures in the yard, fallen
like lizards into a pool

without water, gesticulating and blinking, wiry, slow,
whom I let slowly go

into a house, settle in front of the console and press the remote
to each memory station — pause, hold, mute, flash.

PLASMA

We hear the explosives destroying the weapons,
we see the chemical sky gild the clouds.
Combustible beauty! human shapes, formless cliffs! —
your burning hand in mine,
your gaze, protected and serene,
upon the mountains that disappear
in a calculated flash.
We feel we are saving the globe.
The sun moves in fits.
We have been hiking "for a while."
All that we buried, the waste of
dead, we can now taste the ash of.
Weather above and heat below,
that is adulthood.
It smells like beautiful coastal fog
that doesn't settle out of nor can
be filtered from the traffic
that tears the city.
But we have found our house
like a slender goat a cleft rock,
and it is not ours, it is not habitable
in the old world. A scorpion and an arroyo
suit it now, god on a dead
riverbed. Remember the smallest unit
capable of faith? You bet your life.

Within our small frame, 24 hours and a bit of metabolism.
Speech wounded in a language of love.
The eyeball, the nostril, the anal canal, the earlobe
address certain questions with a gaggle of air.
Most faithful mirror, famous nail.
Isn't this where we made a pass
through one of us, and now we can't remember

which one? Through it spiraled
the very first person who set a light
on the weapons — azure night! I tell you,
from the fumes and bombs you could see everything
instantly weigh nothing. A little fear left over,
oily, rosy, fleshy, the grillwork
of spine and hair. *My youth,* I said, I said,
I'm out of practice. And now we have had to go
all the way back, beyond the moon and the tides,
and it's not some other day or year, it's this
colloidal heart over and over.
There is no other outer space,
and the trees which at one time blossomed
in February have to guess at the season,
the same one. And the fog is chilly despite
the flames, for it is in our heart
we are good, we know the golden staircase
with which to zip our jackets.

INNOCENCE

Fire on the mountain, fire under the lake.
Like children, we look on and dream.
We are loved, and none of the images
for love is absolute, so we are frightened.
We cast a glance into our past,
and not at any remarkable affair
but ordinary efforts — that spray of light
at breakfast where we ran out of milk —
we feel as somehow true.
Dare we touch it with a word
it loses its meaning, though not
its beauty. It becomes a fire
in the heart, incomprehensible and expressive,
an image of the whole, and when finally a man
falls in love with life, it is like an arbor
begged of a desert, for he has accepted
the mirage. Now he is filled with goodness,
as if the unknown were something somehow
slightly slowed, a whole world
in one mountain, pool, and sky
under which we sit sipping milk.
So we are twelve again,
our sexual experience of the world focused
on that tree under which we undress.
The willow caresses us with a sudden gust,
but we have already turned, made up our mind.
It's very cold in the mornings and hot by noon.
Plants grow slowly and never die completely.
Nowhere is there greater sympathy
than between the porcelain sky
and the chlorinated waters of the pools.
Still it stays with us that at any moment

a miracle might enter us as easily.
For we are lucky, we are children
in their fullest expression — lonesome
because we are moving through time
like a dot that becomes a sleeping figure
who is actually dead,
who has been killed,
and from whose nightmare
we continually wake into another
world, a moment we feel like kissing
someone's half-open mouth, once only
an image of fire and water.

FIGURE

Were we to have invested in a figure more distant,
whiter cities, blacker tides, bluer moons?

to have swum at night
as if it were an insufferable day of shade?
Next year gone, missing,
and the sea that damp paper at the extreme.
One hears of eternity rather than remembers.

Like anyone taken by emotion
and chance, the lace and the ice
mountains, we watched the filings from the night
stars razor-part the foam from the water.
Full moons, high wind,
nothing apart from imagining,
a world reduced to a vineyard
beside a cloudy pool.

Tired of flinging our arms back, our faces forward.
Tired of the dive, the save, the pure
form of the verb purpling the hotel where we collapsed
the language of charity,
the final minutes of verse.
After an instant of fulfillment, where's god?
Experience pressed us like a grape.
After forgiveness, we see the earth divided
because the screen in our bedroom shields the rays;
now I see your face in profile (geometry), your hair
in a towel (allegory),
your lips pressed to mine (surface).
There was a fiery scrub, and we were to have survived it,

the worst of which is the bomb blanket.
As for the light that spills off god's glance,
careful records, faithful studies . . .

A peach blushes in bright sunlight, it must be morning.
This is the day fondling
the moon's reflection on the water,
tossing it, smoothing its hair,
babying it.

Are we to invest in a figure more distant,
blacker moons, whiter waters?

SCREENING

A society intent on living in the present tense
likes coming home and doing nothing, but turns on
Entertainment Tonight as a form of literalness,
like seeing someone for the first time
in a photograph, staring at the thing and knowing
our future to be tied to it, shocking, hard to imagine,
hysterically seductive. We don't want to kiss it
or give it a hug, but its presence is purposeful, like a tribe
whose history functions to call our relationships
into question. The situation lacks urgency, yet at the same time
what's public is always so real. We don't therefore have to take
my word for it, we can think of ourselves

as an audience and know all the same we're a view
lit by lightning whose life is imminent, a showcase
of stars just behind what is visible, nothing a small
commercial break can withhold forever.
For a whole moment our lives
are "state of the art," then a mini-transgression
floods in like a nice formal device, someone we bit
when we were a "couple" who now we remember as we rub
lotion on ourselves, home alone, in front of the TV
soaking strawberries in champagne. Relative newcomers
to this part of the country, we feel we can "catch up"
by monitoring the culture in general, seeing what

in particular is different about our new base. Mind you,
we have no intention of "seeing ourselves" in anyone,
but as we refer more and more to our condition as "the surface,"
we have a fear of needing that world, which weighs an amazing ton
and is therefore truer than any symbol, a blazing faceless
instant pressed, as it were, to our lips, threatening
because of our ability not to have to live it

in order to remember. Once you see it played, it's "yours,"
so to speak. This scares us, an everpresent reminder
of limits, a physically perfect world gone to splinter.
The kind of thing that "turns heads" and "stops traffic,"
the model who knows he's gorgeous and can guarantee

he's never been in love, at least not the way we know
love, but rather is "from the place,"
and can infer the wind from the rain, from someone's hands
how long it's going to last, how someone's lips are going
to swell from the feeling really soon, this person
so devoted to self and life is beginning to be an audience
and in no way responsible. Personally speaking, we all
have a spirit that makes it easier to signal with a flame,
and we have a heart that makes it necessary for us to stop
for fresh cherries roadside, but beyond that,
we're indistinguishable from a world filled
to suffocating with "emotion." One touch is like another

as we see it, and the adjustment we made
back there is the one now seen as "perfect" for us then
and "perfect" for someone else now. In fact, we can see
someone doing what we did, watch it cost what it cost
then, we can embrace it fully as "ours," but are we
seeing ourselves or the thing we've made of ourselves,
and are we the same? We say it's getting light out
but cannot say it's late. We seem to be saving
for years for a rug at the foot of the bed, planting the last
marjoram on a balcony in California, but are we enjoying
a false immortality of imagery, the splendor
of moonlessness overlooking a sea?

THE BUTANE EGG

Where once I hummed like a metropolis,
after I saw the bodies there was this feeling
of living in a foreign country, heated and
sealed like a humid summer day, one door away,
the one blown off, and in the middle
of the bridge — where we put it — two huts
painted green. My eyes.

                  My mind wasn't normal,
the sacrifice grew bigger because we feared admitting it,
like having a husband for a minute.

                  Why that feeling has vanished I don't know.
It was a small photograph. I suppose that makes us
                every reason to start with.

The future is a gesture that stimulates
the central nervous system — a new lyricism —
as much theater as you or me,
as once public TV was our projection,
now with an instant's notice
we are each other's project.

Among the few we one day came home bare
to sit by the brazier until the muddy smell
and shell shrunk in a classic calm.
Every time we stand up it seems a toy boat
tips to the left.

                — I've been waiting for you.
                — I'm always floating toward that crooked smile
                                on your face.

Will you be jealous if I tell you about this valley,
about being older, more dead, clearer

in memory? Our brakes squeal
without looking at the accident.

        It's not as if lying in an open
hydrocarbon — the only really feminine thing in my life —
replaces several years in the life of a city.
Cities end like rivers running onto sand.

              Our river —
the umbilical out of the valley —

                  is a copper wire.
On waking, the fuse is irretrievably lit.
Before chronic electricity, we were the ones
who loved the sun most —
now with the last bridge secured
to a dot, the August moon,

              everyone's amphetamine
     is a complex intent.

THE IMPOSSIBLE

I had to give a great speech to a filled hall, beginning
with a flute sonata, and to recite from several books
only two of which I recognized,

which I accomplished, though it took everything out of me
as I tried to hold my posture erect and, failing that,
at least look good on the balls of my feet—this being
nearly impossible, I tried to give the illusion

of weightlessness, or at the very least a sense of rapprochement
with gravity, whereby my head remained light while my heart
suffered and my soul burned,

so that when asked to run, run for all I was worth,
which I tell you was not much by then, because of the pressure
to demur to those around me, cajoling and demanding,
I fled with a kind of verve even I did not foresee
since I was preoccupied with having abandoned a project
it's true only a genius or a madman might have finished
and which I had, frankly, more or less accomplished
by accident, intuition, and a sudden burst of confidence
which shocked even my dearest,

and succeeded in reaching the famous Crystal Springs
heretofore thought to be imaginary, a thing of wonder
but without substance, without substantiation, such blueness
and liquidity, it was unbelievable, but true,
that I stopped on a dime, resisting a personal moment
that surely would have overwhelmed anyone so haunted and
so driven by so many, and experienced what can only be described
as a disappointment, plain and simple, not because the waters
were any less majestic, any less transparent than rumored,

in fact, blue beyond the cerulean of sky over a south
high in the mountains of deepest earth, purpled, nearly black,
that is, if one thought of the sun ever going down
into such waters,

sad because I had never been more in love, more given over
to any one person, place, or thing, and all of existence
seemed paltry next to such feeling, if one did not count
the few stones that uncannily caught my eye, pebbles I
almost smashed out of a euphoria that overcame and nearly
destroyed me — a taste of heavenly winds swept my narrow body,
tickling my ribs with a fancy singing of spirit, tempting,
perfumed — but for the damned six or seven loosely strewn

aforementioned ugly little rocks that buckled my knees
with their gray snaky surface, pimpled, rough, impossibly
connotative, i.e., I saw a thousand lakes in the landscape
of a bird-shat mossy clump glombed to a crag, and bat faces
and bear paws and exoskeletal histories from beyond time,
and so on,

which held me face down, less recalcitrant than I had ever
been, trust me on that, and evermore eager to obey, the longer
I picked out lunar hills and valleys and the more hushed I got
between one ancient, practically moribund, megalith and another,
beamed, so to speak, from oblivion, the body of universe opened
into a gaping mouth

whose lips mercifully shined with the handiwork of creation, or
at least seemed that way to me, by now flattened to the cold
damp floor, reddened with the liveliness of movement, and of
sweat, crimson then, and moving, mouthing something, speaking
in tongues but almost immediately my language, words

I once dared to call, I grant you in a dream, the language
of love, which in this case hastened to particularize itself
in the being of a face, and then the hair and eyes and costume
of beatific figures transsexualized

by ritual and political charioteering such that I no longer
knew myself but rather a consortium of likenesses whose cocksureness
is colloquialized as immediately as the words for it are spoken —
a roaring of motorcycles and then hundreds of faceless, because
one face, hermaphroditic moderns blazed by, upstaging the mono-
chromatic past with theatric mauves and chartreuses, white-faced
and mascara-ed images, eyebrowless, and I found myself in full
color, reproduced electronically, as it were, so eroticized
as to be unreal,

a diorama o'erpowering everything else in common limelight —
dykes on bikes, fag hags, drag queens, steroidal buffs, midnight
blue Black semi-nudes, boytoys, unzipped sado-masochistic
six-foot tricks, the semi-erect, the innocent, in gym shorts
and in slips, tuxedos, T-shirts and cut-offs, jeans impaled
at the crotch — godly, larger-than-life meaning assigned
to them by messages spelled out on their chests, "Silence
Equals Death," etc., until, so engorged, their numbers blur
into a mass of energy that finally disperses into the missions
and the tenderloins from whence they came, into the planetary
city named irreverently and made familiar by necessity,
"sex,"

and I passed out onto those innocuous stones, trifles
I might have missed another day, waking to stumble
between two destinations, home or on, knowing I
had forgotten — o alcatrazed face, betrayed,
abandoned! — more than any metaphor provided

because it too is ultimately betrayed and abandoned,
forgotten life because of this paper face, this alphabet
and these blanks I trusted, naturally, like a form
of breathing, life I have to return to which I made

more difficult than walking off the globe
by imagining I had to say a few tired words
into an ear, near-empty auditorium . . . beginning
with a couple of scratched notes, only some of which
I'd actually written . . .

BEAUTY

Everyone around us was called "Missing,"
a hundred countries testified
but we tried not to forget,
desperate not to forget to remember,
because in a poem
the truth doesn't have one time or place,
not a relative, or even a body.
I know I am separate and I got here
by love's lower lip, pulled from a song
into this world. If He is pulled
from your bed, you can believe
nothing comes from nothing.
Because we were happy we were lucky
someone had written a few words
about your hair in a twist
and mine curling, parted,
our necks like Greek columns,
swans in a floating world.
We mustn't lose
count — every mountain must be given
back pinecones, every ravine
its stones, cottonwoods
their streams, poplars their. . . .
Even if it hurts to look at god
in a form we admire.

BLANKS FOR NEW THINGS

She wondered how to make the new faithful to the original.
Everything seemed so much itself, and already something else.

Life became thicker and thicker over time. My fidelities to her
and to the whole place became extremities of the same god.

While she heard voices I was swooning, there was this seduction
by the shells, the stones, the wind, aided by our thirst. Now

there is more than the protagonist and the foil, there's material
in a visual shuffle. This is our perfect life, she said, and said,

I would do it again. It's a narrative which concerns itself
with the events of five minutes, missing April or December.

All of a sudden you're in real time. She puts her arm around me, to
comfort me, while I'm stuck.

Eight evenings of the heavens burning. Do we make a pact?
I'm pure space, you be the battleground. Horrors, of the kind

after summer when vines entangle your ankles, grapes pucker
your lips; I'm not going to play in the game, I think I know

when I thought I said I was thinking of talking to you.
Not to remember would be more painful.

You think you're going to be with your dog after the war.
Don't take time so personally.

THE GENERAL'S BRIEFING

Here is the infant formula plant
missed by a hair's breath next to it
here is the biological research facility
bombed with advanced machinery
of pinpoint accuracy

Here are the small women and large babies
the medium-sized women with tiny children
and the large, the tall women with shrinking babies
and here are the former apartments and the former
neighborhoods and here is the dirty famous polluted well-known
historically besieged important river that ran
the commerce, throbbing in the belly of the city

Here are the candlesticks of the mosque
here are the pre-dawn musicians
here is dawn
here is the all clear
here are the radio waves
here are the telecommunication antennae
here are the rats
here are the fires
here is the dysentery
here is the one doctor
here is the vial of medicine for the population
here is the international community to rebuild the city
here finally is the city
the dry faucet the endless alloy pipe
the rose plume over the scarlet plume over the yellow plume over
the charcoal over the flames

Here is the eyewitness
here are his notes his swollen pad

here his toothmarked lead pencil
his presspass his signature

here are the letters of his whole name
here are the vowels separating from the rest
here the tender "e" the demanding "u" the sorry "o"
and the "a" and "i" suddenly very close intimate in fact
given the circumstances of no air no water no electricity
no society no geography no say no information no

here is the audience the couch soiled the telephone
wired to the living room the Super Bowl on TV
the background of epic winter sky the letters recycled
practice jets the speed of sound the traffic Sunday
shoppers with their imported and domestic cars
tuned to the war

the clerk at Circle K
tuned to the war
the anti-war demonstrators with their headsets
tuned to the war
the Super Bowl commentators making an exorbitant fee
tuned to the war
the police guarding the stadium
the FBI routing out possible terrorists
the boys growing mustaches to be terrorists
the terrorist feeling death's high

Here is the answer here is the Pope the minister the President
the representative of the people here is the student the official
here is the quarterback here is the servant here here

Monday night—don't you see us on the shelled road,
out of gas, without our masks, money, without our credentials,
we sense you, your eye on the high-tech telescope, as one
throws back his stringy hair from his forehead,
another rubs her throat, waking it—the only thing
missing from your screen, your vision, out of earshot
the smell of so-called immortal souls, immortal earth,
fruit ripened, ready for market,
baths ended abruptly, weeks ago, the last of the drinking water,
the only thing missing from your enormous awareness
the smell—as when one meets the great love of his life, the same
yellow hair she imagined the very same speech same touch same
upturned lips, and cannot—
the smell—as when one hears her child and cannot—
the smell—who has slept all night, the sheets cold & wet—
the smell—silence suddenly, electronic, professional, governmental
silence—
the smell—whitewashed walls on all sides, infinite—
the smell—desert trenches, a face, a leg—
the smell—red hills, anxiety, our heads held up on sticks

as I speak from a third-floor room the smell
throughout the city the country the region
carnal diarrhea & vegetal puke & mineral dry heave
no salt for tears no sea for sewage—

ON THE ISLAND

A sound close to the ear.
What am I going to do for the war?
I'm going to stop it—.

Why is it they took centuries for what now takes an hour,
and we have to hurry?
On the island, everything is made of stone.
Why is it they worshipped for centuries
what now takes an hour,
and we have to lift them into place ourselves?

We should collaborate with machines, so we're looking for some.
Every afternoon I'm in the alkaline of dream, or so it seems
to be afternoon, that is Your light, isn't it,
among the roses?

This invisibility of mine, why do You welcome it so?
I don't want to be known by what You do,

moving at dangerously slow speeds
as if this were a landscape after the extinction of being.

In which case it is possible to avoid, easier
than the shooting from the roofs on the Ramblas, 1930's,
at one's own people.

On the island, the military smiles at the civilians
(on a point of no importance, there is always documentation).

Why is it the present completely absorbs us like real estate?
In the dream of the island,
houses shake down into pebble and sand.

One thing I'm not going to do, I'm not going to wave madly,
my newlywed, when they're hurled at our shield.
I'm going to hold to my first 30 seconds in hell—

grim despite its young age—
and when we open my eyes,
apricot trees a foot high between rows of tiny new potatoes.

THE HEALING FOUNTAINS

My last unnatural day began
on top of somebody, loosely speaking,

who was screaming about the dark times.
I realized that whether you pose Rose, or Rose poses,

it's prose.
So I finally said to myself, that's not a life, that's a dancefloor,

and those aren't lips, you asshole, that's *lipstick*.
The flesh itself,

it's not exact, it's precise,
skin and blood,

that thundercloud whose lightning pierced my soul.
That fake schedule of the future, too full of Fridays,

had the fish hopping mad about it.
All the while working love with a migraine,

they nonetheless swam, just an option, not a destiny,
toward the healing fountains

because they cared, not for me,
but for the woman I would become,

and all their large, magnified underwater bodies
never spoke, of course,

but had the right language bent out of shape
so I finally heard

you tell me you love me, in my ear like
on the phone because I couldn't see you.

There was never a home, with my old lovers in midair it was
different finally to find their place in the sun,

as you said, Lord Jesus of Nazareth,
completing another action. Which reminds me,

I appreciate that you are more
than halfway done

with the creation of the world, because now that we are closer
to forever, the poem has enough time

to demand the sequence cast aside.
In other words it's a shock

to love someone else entirely.

POINT OF DEPARTURE

We never thought pleasure in the detached world
would be as much as a grain of salt or sand.
When we were young, yesterday,
one foot after another on your day off,
we went straight from the movies to the seashore
knowing art and life were separate, friendly,
and if the streamwater wasn't fit to drink —
I cup my hands now, thinking of love —
it was cool and a symbol, music came from it,
and the elk poisoned themselves only a little —
after a hundred years' absence a small price.

This late in the day,
a cliff and waterfall below us in heaven,
elk ghost the laurel and chaparral
of the Point Reyes coast,
fogged in, an adaptation for our time
as one might imagine an air-conditioned desert
to have been.
We are saturated in thought
as once with light
anyone could walk six miles easily on the sky road.
Still equal to the life which called them forth,
the tule elk churn opposite the blocked sun,
                    freak children
of the universe, feeling its size as comprehensible.

                    No relationship beyond that though —
the California shore is alone on earth
along the San Andreas fault,
as a snake on my property once
gone has a presence.
Life only imagined hurts,

that's why we're still here in the painless eucalyptus air,
invisible, night and day indivisible. We're left
with some things hardly alive
                    among gods, questions, awe—
how is my life with a stranger from this world?

NEW BODY

There's a sort of eternity
when we're in bed together
whether silently you awaken
me with the flat of your hand
or sleep breathing with a small scratch
in your throat, or quietly attach
a bird to the sky I dream
as a way in to my body —

Now you have made me excited
to accept heaven as an idea
inside us, perpetual
waters, because you let yourself
fall from a sky you invented
to a sea I vaulted
when it was small rain
accumulating — My heart drained

there and fills now in time
to sketch in the entire
desert landscape we remember
as an ocean port,
that part of me accepting
your trust, a deep
voluptuous thrust into my hours,
that has no earthly power

but lives believing you were made for me
to give in to completely,
every entry into you the lip

of water that is in itself scant hope
broken into like sleep
by kisses — Policed in the desert
by a shooting star, we are the subversive
love scratched out of sky, o my visitor.

EXPERIENCE

Those who had wanted to feel more
at home on the globe,
and those to whom so much happened
met, because fate won't reminisce,
fate deposits the incongruous
like oil in the sea,
which was fought for bitterly.
For everyone wanted to be different
and better. We sweated
the sickness of the self,
as a whale will give up in one puke
the essence of perfume to a stranger.
Daisies which smelled a little
more than nothing on earth
press my heart now, I remember how
young I was, lifting them
through the Great Hall.
Only making love to you wasn't I
curious about the rest of experience.

WITH THE WORLD

I would like to finish
a computer project, or one stinking letter
for work, or menu for lunch,
even before that,
to get to market
as they unload tomatoes—
organic, from Nogales—nowhere
sweeter for January, young, fleshy.

I would like to convince an acquaintance
I am better now that the drama
between me and my lover is over,
a truce, if I may say so,
regarding our long-standing feud.
We shook in a restaurant, that is, we cried,
and cut the fish, forcing a lemon.
A pity, we said, we were still eating
from the sea, not quite like slaughtering
a cow, but nonetheless obscene.
Then we paid too much,
saying it was worth it.
Later I thought about worth,
and couldn't finish, the phone sounded
and the sky split with practice jets
despite the distance of the war
around a corner of the globe.
A meteorologist swelled one in her hand
on the TV—I had her on "mute"—
as meanwhile I failed to persuade
my acquaintance—of anything, in fact—
hanging up on her, inside, shut tight,
registering the report on winter desert
weather, dry and hot, very dry and hot, not

at night, at night the unexpected daily cold,
again dry, cold dry winds, a little
dry, cold, sandy, empty wind.

Next the reporter from the front,
that desert very much
like mine in Tucson, where they train,
dry and hot, then at night, generally
quiet, cold. The picture punctuates
with Scud fire and Patriot interception,
except when the American system fails
and the Russian system (categorically
no longer the enemy), lights
the sky, the apartment building
cinder slightly bluer on cable TV.
Or am I imagining seeing the attack,
seeing the attack the next day? A dry
voice crackles, garbled like a forties evening
over radio waves, a nasal traditional
Hebrew song droning without instrument,
strangely pagan and Appalachian, a cry
rattling in the cavity of a dulcimer,
like an empty, once lived-in apartment.
(If only I could remember the story,
the year?, _____ goes out for some pears,
with only her purse and a cardigan, a
little dress, gets picked up by Germans and never
returns again, lands up in Israel, no one
has heard of her, a poet, somebody's lover).

I would like to finish listening
to the war, to sit alone another hour
with my aging remote and follow

updates from the leaders of the free world,
ours, of course, and from them
infer advice—it's not impossible—about
my life, the casualties of love,
albeit the analogy is damned inappropriate,
I cannot help a personal moment, petty, yet
I would like to finish the narrative,
or at least be allowed to go back, perhaps
merely for lunch, having shopped outdoors,
the weather perfect, cool late into morning,
sealed my exemplary work into envelopes,
quarreled, turned my acquaintance
into a friend, yes, to be able to return,
burst a couple of tomatoes—a happy accident—
while confiscating the best, young, fleshy,
only a little purple, bruises I can accommodate,
practically deny if I turn them underside.

Creon decrees that Polynices, who led an attack
against the city, shall be left unburned,
"carrion for the birds to tear,
an obscenity for the citizens to behold."
Outside the city, pecan and lemon trees
wait for rain—rain would be untimely,
but they know nothing of that—
it happens, bad weather, reconnaissance
can't make out the damage to the front.
Oil fields on fire, lemons in fog,
which drop onto dead-of-night moss,
gone by dawn. One picks his teeth,
thinking he's off-camera.

FALSE GODS

We were whispering because the sound carried.
Things molten remembered the reeds and woods,
and where blossoms and berries survived,
people gathered to dream that dream together.
We sat with our backs to the Mediterranean sun
that couldn't set. Chimes — like I often thought
of turning to see you for I sensed that love
was possible, so near. But it was clear
you were in another world, and loving the earth
as you did I felt like god
because I'd simply gone, simply acquiesced,
who was prone anyway to reminisce.
We used the few words left over
and over. Your body blushed of circumstance
not scorched by one last blossom.
Meanwhile your golden hair flickered.
There were promises.

EXPOSURE

There was the shock — and delay — of seeing them
from the back, drying off and disappearing like ice
in a cold drink in the sun. For it was summer,
all the adrenalin of the sun and no one thought
to intercept them.
                          So our older bodies fade.
We leave the shadows where they belong —
there are more important things to endure
than one's own darkness, anchored to the ground
like a strange musical instrument. The wind played,

the sun burned my bearings. The beach was a godsend.
After not seeing you for a long time, only this
island turned, the static surface like earth itself
now circumstantial, adrift — .

Though I move dramatically close, we don't kiss,
our faces timeless without their original sin.
In the past, the new world begins to darken again.
In the future, nothing stops me from going in.

COUPLING

Adolescent Bacchus in his grape wreath lies semi-
sheathed in front of a bowl of figs, grapes, pears,

apples & a loose peach, & his eyebrows are penciled in
for all the world to see he is a god & real, sexy,

muscular & with a summer paunch, late summer, patches
out a window of hay & green fields what he is

perhaps looking at, so unchanged is the scheme & always
drawn to human scale, posing in a dank basement to get

the shading right, so the summer is all in his dark
round eyes: if your silken skin can stand

another bite, plump evening, it will not show on his body,
his right nipple left of center so nearly perfect we are

mirrored there; Art fusses & the pool of wine in the hand-
blown carafe won't blink, nor will his offer of a taste

held out to you change you in the head, because in fact
he may be showing you what he's about to sip & never

share; I hate to think what you are doing now, over there,
gone from me as distantly as a century in a world that lifts

its taboos more easily than we ever wanted to
lift my body off of you, in other words, never, typically

a day & night, my idea about love misshapen into a sound, no,
into an argument or a story I forget, I've had a rough night

with the power cut, hours of pounding in a bowl of mountain
thunder, eyeballing this medieval town illumined by the oldest

trick in the book, god's theatrics like a drunk lit from within
coursing a way home across the pitched sky; a blessing

upon your sun-drenched August morning, your former furnace-
blasted city gone middle management into computer lines

while I prepare to leave my own adopted alien culture, a
burning reduced to a smell inside a memory inspired

by a word like "hay" or "sunflower" & not the other
way around, as Proust thought — it starts in the abstract

& races to the heart like lightning to an apple bough
in a pastoral, love, a scene, darling, wherein one person

cuts into another with a disdain borne out of the past
& recreated in the present as if it were real, causal,

a subject open to criticism, interpretation, theory, preference;
so you hate me now too, as then

in a sweaty room so electrified together we had to be
shouldered out of that world, black & blued

to be spared a fire whose flame tips came
too close to the truth: our father who art

in heaven & not in his right bed
puts out the cigarette & tires of his glory; now that you are free

& have done with me without so much
as lifting a finger & I imagine

happier for it, red buttocked by the lake of your youth
where it is safe to say we were a nightmare, a match

in a haystack, it is here meanwhile they've had to plant
the ubiquitous sunflower for the oil lost during a freeze

of their famed olive groves, a country brought to its knees
making of woe a supplication & a remedy; they say

Caravaggio killed somebody & anyway was a pagan & a homo-
sexual; if you put a coin in a metal box a 20 watt bulb comes on

for 5 minutes in a cold corner of a church & up rises one
of his portraits tourists in a dozen languages crush in

to view until the light cuts & no one budges, massed in the
cave staring at the eye socket which remains; someone then

has to cough up the change or forget about it, it's always
the same, too cheap or stupid, too passive, until some lame

bystander catches on, & the burning lasts forever for another
5 minutes, all eyes tortured to the wall, the characters

that live on the wall, in the paint, in a stable or
what have you, a reflection of universal law; they seem real,

stopped forever proffering red wine in the lake
of some long-stemmed glass, say, with a crown of late summer

purplish grapes & autumn leaves; an adolescent
with a woman's face & a man's boyish hairless chest,

a killer perhaps, & certainly a drunk & a queer or whatever,
just the same, someone somebody or some several

knew intimately, by the stained teeth & weathered hair,
so real you could lick the flesh like a cat

daydreaming over cream with a thoughtless expression,
like when you're thinking or think you're thinking

about those too distant to be made out coupling in a field
of freshly-mown hay, a thousand eyes of sunflowers on them.

CAST FROM HEAVEN

There must have been something like writing across their faces.
There would have been sorrow, and tenderness, would there not?
And a sound, as if someone, I don't know by what means, spoke
our first thoughts upon waking.
We won't see them again, vagrants, skins.
A rash of daylight.

Careful. Time pairs with nature,
time is evil and sentimental.
One vital expression will return you to the creamery for your fill
and it will be farther and farther away,
no longer part of the country but deep in the bowel
of the city, which is all but framed in memory.
A few spires, girders extended into space,
and beyond, sky, where the sun stamped everything for deportation.

Once there was a choice, to talk or not, to boast,
to stall, we accepted it; but now, cast from heaven
the few words correspond only to ideas, and cannot help us
spend the night. Here's a man,

let's watch him and learn what he thought,
separated from his child, who chose her mother
when there was no difference.
He said, *God,* and it sounded
like *what?*
and like *stop.*
We mustn't let go the mother and child simply
because they wished to point at the sky.
What is the sense at the end?

The greasy soap bubbles where the creamery drained into a lake,
The grease-spot of the lake into the sky.

We sit around the fire.
Military terminology, slang, specific reference to
recent books, a grunt — those awake
meditate on the long night
while the sleeping dream dawn.
Thus work and rest are shared.

MARIN HEADLAND

Grief as we know it
and pity as we know it,
the roaring foggy darkness as we know it,
love as we know it
and beauty and magnetism,
energy, as we know it,
as we have come to know it, relationship
and intimacy, as we know,
the great earthquake, life, as we know it,
tension, destiny, family,
movement at the subtlest level of function, as we know it,
human beings as we know them,

California, the blue dolphin,
the eucalyptus, the umbrella pine, the coastline,
as we have come to know them,
the mist, the lovers, the children,
the aging, the homebound, the irreversible,
these, as we have come to know them, the homosexual's parade,
the mayor's limousine, the homeless's cape of newspaper,
as we call them, our plate of food our rings our fresh haircuts
our meager donation our writers our poetry as we have come to know it
our education our manner our estate our transportation our travel
our privacy our privilege as we have come to know it our sexuality
our vision as we know it

lightning as it is known, plants, peaches, wine,
failure, esteem, faith,
the future, as it is known, the noun,
as we have come to know it,
a "thought" as we know it, a "commitment" a "vote" a "religion"
as we know them,
ghosts, tempests, gods — the days, the instances,

the dream, as we know it, the poetic, the pacific, the allegorical,
the excuse, as we know it, the error,
the meaning, as we have come to know it, far away,
as we have come to know it, death, as we know,
heaven as it is known, and timelessness and grace, as is
expected to know, and as we have come to,

loathing, avarice,
a drink, a safety net, a parent, a dog, a weapon, a
response, a paddle, a marine, a debutante, a quarter,
a parasite, without knowing it, a minor actor, a case in point,
a husband, a weekend, without knowing, an admission,
a clue, without knowing, a country, a pope,

land rights, tenants, garages, inventory,
without knowing them, a twenty-seven year old, without knowing it,
it, itself, them, themselves,
as we know without knowing

private parties with ribs barbequed, embroidery of dead names,
the state of Russian music, the modern sensibility, as it is known,
the telecommunications network, the criminal element, as they are
known, the "wall," the "bomb," the "communist," the "TV," the "free,"
as they are variously known
and now me, without knowing, as is generally known,
me, as the sea and sky appear to know without knowing,
and you, knowing full well, without knowing,

"plump girls pinched with butter," "babies with roses and baby roses,"
January, February, June and July,
lipstick and blood, as they are associated and known,

as we have come to know our home, our place, our time, our
hour, our
favorite,
dark beach as we have come to,

in agreement, with little else to say, as a matter of course,
silenced, not a moment too soon, without further ado, without
a word in edgewise

the mere mention of three in the afternoon, a Tuesday in summer,
memories, as they are variously known
and were to have been understood and, commonly, forgiven,
this choice and those images and that situation
and this conclusion,
these approximations and those generalizations, as we know
and fear them,
as is our nature, toothy, hairy, spiny,

a faultline of carmine poppies, raspberries,
spring green gullies, grasses
and ravens,
a place never seen, the imagination as we know it,
bugless and treeless and airless and waterless and sunless.

BY NATURE

If it could be, it would be 7 o'clock.
Two men who have all day
been picking peaches and pears
go back through the rows
for the fallen and pecked fruit
left for dead.
They take them for themselves,
filling the wire baskets of their motorbikes.
They light cigarettes
and pedal their engines to a running start.
Then an unexpected thing.
It cannot even be said
the sun resists setting —
in itself still something —
the sky behind it so recently
darkening "brightens"
but only by my recollection.
I surprise myself
with an angry thought
I'm as far away as you
make me, you shit
about my lover,
whom I had until this moment
the option of missing.
When I understood my being
half a globe away,
I assumed I could get there in time.
The earth is now
like a fruit a human
has knifed,
tumbling fruitlessly
through space.
You notice when you finally stop

running through your day,
at table, the dizziness,
the blown earth in the red wine.
And the constant
bruising as we fall up,
like falling out of love
where you are suddenly free,
terribly guilty
without caring.
No longer is there a single self
but a whole host
of opposition, completely random
pellets and debris,
mistresses and masters of the universe,
who will be there for you I promise, always.

MORE OR LESS A SORROW

What do I see? The lightless past.
It's talk. It kept us going
between lovemaking. And while I was not you
I discovered how truly fascinating you were,
bleaching your hair and removing your underwear
for me as much as for you, gestures I took
seriously all the way back to their beginnings
in parody and on TV. But
after we went all that way I found a heart
on a stick, hopping among the fresh desert
sage, and even then it was great
to be alone. Somewhere between the middle
and the end of our long talk we ended
up inside, touched but never seen
which we must have had trouble believing in,
tender as it was, otherworldly, like an idea
finally devoid of meaning, the pure feeling
of coming outdoors, finding no one watching,
nothing moving in the steady wind.
The rest of the time I felt was always
a premonition of my first night alone,
the phantom hotel of my forties,
this helpless country. If ever I was ready
to live a life, by evening
what have I done? I hurt you, all over
nothing, a trifle, as things go. Noise
on the brain, habitually tooled
to the point it drove us practically
insane, and we had to notice, I suppose,
that inside this world
is another more — it must have to do
with our placement — full of people

with questions rather than choices.
There I found you experience
through your heart and soul—very noble—
while I experience through my nights and days,
a vague union—maybe it'll save me,
maybe it's a waste—

DESERT ABSTRACT

It might have been a little different,
                                    your hair auburn or brown, longish,
torn about by a rip-wind,
                         high tide, the muffled pounding deafening,
an explosion in a pillow
                       emblazoned on my face like a like
a lie invading a smile
                   blood coming in on a northeaster,
                                         our steamy souls
destined for the plates of gods,
                        an indestructible hour
of suffering like gods
                   after they have eaten and been surprised
by their slaves and skewered
                     screaming "history now" "destiny now"
everyone wanting a little quiet
                     in the end, a kind of reserve
following the buck and resound
                       of our finally pouring our hearts out,
                 our wharf rats and moon slag hosed down
                   for white space
which regrets nothing
               is not guilty
                   and reprimands the violets
we hydrate by whispers by real feelings by tears,
              showering a desert on eternity

POETRY

Invited onto the grounds of the god,
who decides what words mean,
we are amazed at the world
perfect at last. Gold fish, gold finches, gold watches,
trash blasted into crystal, all
twilights supporting one final sunset
with slender fingers of consolation.
A little reality goes a long way,
far off in the distance the weak sea
beaches its blue whales, the small sky
melds the stars into one
serious fire, burning eternally
out of control, our earth.
But here we are visiting
the plutonium factory dazzling
to the eye, the one good one remaining
to us in our wisdom. We have concluded
that automatic, volcanic sunrises and sunsets
where light trips on the same cardboard vine
are blinding, and we would rather fail
painfully slowly than survive a copy
of the world perfect at last. Yet we are
impressed by the real thing, which we walk
like dew upon flesh, suddenly lubricated and translucent
beyond our dreamiest desires, hard-pressed
to object. Consoled that there is so little
difference between the terrible and the real,
we admire the powerful appleseeds bobbing
in the dewy pools, we cannot help
but enjoy their greeny spring, and it is only by resting

on the miraculous grass, wildly uniform, mildly serene,
that we sense
with our secret selves, the little bit we left behind and
remember, that we are out of our element, that we are
being made into words even as we speak.

ADORATION

Now I have come from the Berg String Quartet Opus 3
performed by the Young Artists of the Taos School
home in a sperm of rain
that declares itself to the loaded fireplace
as dead as the world last Friday
though god knows there is a drought in every other state
we live by voices we shall never hear.

May the violent haystack consuming himself as a young man
(that night I went misshapenly to witness the Los Angeles Lakers)
be eaten off the table by the broadening sun
and not the barkeep who bloodies the evening steak.
He was not soundlessly spilling his Miller
onto a manufactured Mexican teen, but I saw and was
hoarse by the time he will reach her alarm

under the stars' neon shoes, stepping lightly over the firmament
of Oglivie's where the plane trees yellow the margaritas
of the yellow moon behind them, and the brown moon of rain drowns
the elbow moon of that face coming closer to crumbling
before we can choose, before we can announce there is a choice,
before we can prove there is, there was.
I have a handle on my jeans where I would provide

that turn in the town where the tourists meet the art trade
for the firewood they will burn next winter
while skiers fly overhead in an enforced frieze,
a bride a minute beholding Agua Fria Peak in her Angel Fire
T-shirt, while her husband ejaculates from an Air Force jet,
where once there were a few now many,
once a hundred now a state of collapse, a couple of

dogs who pitch and yaw all night for a little water.
For now is the opening the art world belittled, the V-neck and
the bedspread, the stockinged leg, the chain and gear
makeup, the turquoise that lights the lights of the lights
that are lit, our souls nippled with antennae so the world will
hear, the party will know we were the ones who trained like mad to
do it, do it, do it in the perforated gleam of the dollhouse window.

GOD FROM A MACHINE

You put your hands on her waist, but you are in another world. The world is small and you see it arranged in simplified angles and diagonals, in heights and lines, steeples and domes. Space is not foreshortened or compromised in any way except the whole, entirely reproduced with the knowledge that it is a suggestive world. Out on the newly cleansed avenues, glossy windows like magazine covers, gentle folk glide on course like soldiers, and we enter with a view of these broad "Hitlerian" promenades and a Great Hall of the Reich rising to a quarter of a kilometer. The dome itself could fit St. Peter's into it sixteen times; on certain days its top is lost in low homogenous clouds.

This architecture is central to a conception of ourselves in simple geometries, grossly amplified, reduced to a view; nothing could be more computable. Take the scene where you move up the Avenue of Victory and go into your hotel to make love. Our computer, with a simple algorithm, will hold a mathematical model of the vast thoroughfare while you figure how much we see of the splendid "granites" and the leafless "chestnut trees" through your eyes, the windows of our tour bus.

Once through the symmetrical lobby and into the hotel, the rendering becomes more difficult, the more decorative the balustrades and velvet folds of light-resistant curtains become, the more raised the ticklish pattern on the bedspread, the more billowy a shower curtain, the more tiered the tinkling lighting. Most difficult of all to conceive, to engineer, the miniature man and woman carved of chocolate who sleep on a silver tray beside your bed. You sit and strip off your sharply pressed pants, whose recently acquired unreplicable creases mock all effort at perfection.

All accoutrements, personal and institutional, profoundly affect

seduction, as you well know. Hearing her, you contrive a dark-
ness with a mere touch of a switch, erasing any further doubt
about appearances, erasing all visual distinction between virtual
and real, and "it happens," i.e., you sense she's near. She joins
you from her orderly world into your hybrid, adopted culture,
but as soon as you embrace her waist, this scenic rendezvous resu-
mes on her terms, her spongy flesh, her doughy, lumpy, plush,
mossy rural scene,

hairy, spiny, calcic, enameled, and pitted. Now you feel your
way, unsure in the messy darkness you trip over, breaking a
fluted glass, nearly certain she's left the last of her lipstick on you.
You swipe your face with the back of your hand. Maybe it's bet-
ter to see for yourself, in the world you've created. Better in the
virtual light of your invention. So like a god from a machine, you
wrestle to that light. Probably she doesn't love you. And she cer-
tainly doesn't stop there, at the borders of what you conceive as
the affair. Rather, she raises the curtain on the vistas below, and
you have to watch yourself on any island she cares to point out,
passing a spark of divinity with her ordinary finger able, it seems,
to move through glass, through the grid so carefully designed by
you, every individual flicker reflecting appropriately in the eyes
of your beloved, in mirrors, and off the marble pillars of your per-
spective. You see, peripatetically, alternately:

Islands

*You attend an opera in an amphitheater where it pours several hours, and
you sit because you have paid to see the morality play,* Don Giovanni,
*on stiff outdoor chairs, like airport rows, in borrowed oilcloth and hood,
until the circle tightens around the leading rat and, certain of his guilt, you
exit. You give your ticket to a girl in the same rain outside the stadium,
and drive home with the heat on, not thinking of her again.*

You stand expressionless in a long coat on a ninth floor balcony, to the east you can see the fragile glassworks and, beyond them, pipes coughing steam. Below it has snowed, and only a boy with a white dog and a dark collar on a long chain and an old man walking a bicycle appear, hurrying, the old man talking to the street and the boy slipping. You drum the metal rail before going in, thinking this occasion will never come again. Traffic crawls and puffs. The red stoplight has a halo. When you step back in, she threatens to leave you, but does not leave you.

Late one long summer day, by evening, you go swimming. A young tired couple on lounges listens to the radio. Lightning far away, far enough not to matter. A kid bangs his fist on the Pepsi machine for his change, loses it, averts everyone's eyes, goes back out the fire gate. A guy is standing in the pool, smoking. You do a few laps on your back, then the crawl, which you learned long ago, not getting the breathing right. You have a nice body but move slowly. A man and a woman talk loudly in an apartment nearby, making love, you realize, the woman's laughter more serious, then rhythmic. A moment of your first passion flashes, kissing her teeth and lipstick in the darkness, tasting the lipstick. You swim another lap, missing the wall on your flip. By now it is dark. When you towel off, you smell the skin of your arm mixed with chlorine.

One day you get a call from a woman you knew well ten years ago, or so. You're determined not to compare her fearlessness to despair, for fear it's your despair. It's a coincidence she's here without your thinking of her, same power you were drawn to then that she couldn't channel into love you couldn't give. Each young body dead is still alive in the other, as you run from an ancient storm, slamming a screen and falling nightly to the floor. That boundary there, where she cannot see you older as you shower, your back to the water, washing your hair—would it be a relief to see her now and show your face? But your fate is to rid yourself of history without the benefit of the present, the fault lines on your foreheads, your hearts—you have to live in a world you dismantle because you in-

vented it, starting now, you think about making love in the daytime, the
heat at its height.

All this sounds familiar. You remember promising to advance, to love better, to attend to matters. You always had to be reminded but then failed. There it is, an emotional, physical thing, like being spooked in some amusement park on a sticky summer afternoon with a few strangers. Or jammed into some inner night without end, lights, smoke, fires, a subway car of sweating bodies. Now you gaze upon the threshold of the past and the other, infinitely reassuring world of total recall and correction. Memory and desire on the one hand, and electronic retrieval and fulfillment on the other. Life, or an afterlife of functions and rewards. Many painful versions or one enhanced, permanent vision. A past you are responsible for no matter how you figure it, or a present you can trust. There's hardly a choice; in fact, it's made for you. You watch it like television or a movie. You have become comfortable.

Your world is beautiful. You're virtually alone. You turn your back on the mad beepings of the jungle, the walled cities, and the dreary seas. How serene! The curve of the earth is palpable. You lie flat, you stand tall. You know yourself and your place in the universe. Lost days seem to you now retrieved, the broad-brimmed hat of your youth, and those loud songs, and the apartments at the end of the century, white couches and patterned rugs. Visible, too, are the vast greens of yesterday as they swelled into the wall-to-wall future, four-dimensional, philosophical, recreations more glorious and solid

than the events themselves, which you once gripped and twisted into oblivion. These waftings and dreams return fully, you regard them now with a greater eye — ethereal walks through the park, under the heavy dying boughs, into the tiny restaurant where you could see the stuffed fish and ribbons of food prepared, the bread steamy. And you're not dead, not dying. You're in a false and steady state, unafraid. Now you can really laugh at the day you interviewed poorly, and cry over the grave of your friend. Now you can feel the rain, raining everywhere, wherever it seems right, and take the heat, and swim to shore powerfully; now you can eat ravenously, sleep like a baby, and make love with your whole body.

SEQUEL

You are in hell. You've fallen from a universe of sodden valleys and mountains of rare verdure, steel and cement roadways, ballooning stadiums, fallen into a world of play like a match struck brightly in a room without gravity. You are on the side of silence that has a background hum, in a neo-green light once thought to represent the sea, but now a reflection, literally, an idea. Today you can "bend metal" or "split" the "invisible" "whenever," and you're indistinguishable from the thing you seek for the life beyond your perpetually lit screen, a cure, if you will.

Let a squiggle represent a house with two or three pines. Let a dot represent your twenty-year-old body. Let a curve be a place of dark streets, early morning, a scent of hot apples. Let the illusion of time be a woman racing in heels on smooth stones for a train. Let the numbers of rivers and creeks and puddles be the rivers and creeks and puddles. Let the fatigue-green canopy be the powder-blue sky. Let the light darken slowly, into vermilion and lavender. Let the perfect erect structures stand for the slender rusty skyline. Let the smoke rise, over the screams of birds.

We see it is difficult. We see you struggle effortlessly "forever." You're all we have. We have a feeling for the future you left behind, we've dreamt you climbing out, and have seen one leg dangling precipitously over the edge, like a limb severed in a war, with your pant and sock and shoe, just as you left them, scruffy and stylish. Let that console you. Though you were drawn into a constant season, we remember you were confused, we remember how you loved to be touched, how you grabbed the browning leaves and the soggy lilies, and cursed the nettles and bled with your face in the roses. Though you were a coward, we haven't your courage now. The thought of you returning in a heavenly glow, your equations complete . . . We trust you, even if we can only sense you. We know you're one of us.

INTO A SPACE MY TIME HAS GONE

Dreams never stop, I simply rise
and shower and cook breakfast in the light
of the flares. Then I go forward, the liquid
teeming with hatching fish. We're lying comfortably
on our backs, how we best get along,
yet when I wake I'm all alone.
It never fails,
we find the single most beautiful
tree laden with ornamental fruit.
A poetic obsession, nothing
to return to the world,
were we going there. As it happens,
we name the world with a word in mind,
and then locate the thing in the leaves.
It is some remote horizon we move closer.
This hard work is love and it's funny
to be back. It's *like* I'm not here,
but with all the porches and pigs in pickups,
the stink of it and the roar which are fake
fit under the sun and feel ok.
Endless search through earthy shades,
orange tones, octagonal street designs,
freeways of apparently black construction trucks,
mad beeping in the high-tones of the jungle,
and the airport that cages our dreams
hangs dimly in memory,
who turns into a child.

CALIENTE

So I shut off the light and listened to the rain.
It finally cooled things down.
I'd swum,
& gotten something to eat, couscous,
a carrot, and then settled in,
naked, early,
and had nothing to do so
turned on the radio,
an ordinary lyrical solo,
and on
into evening, gratifying,
lonely, the steady
downpour broken with thunder,
lightning stumbling
& limbs crisscrossing the sky
now pearl,
willow, cherry & aspen
heavy, a credible
time to remember other rain,
but I didn't for more
than a moment test myself
against your favorite season
breaking seamlessly in,
and only a little dreamt your skin
characteristically floating on mine
(forgive me a memory of coastal Spain,
misty red grapes —

ORBITLESS

For one white tulip, and a dark iris with a heart of yellow . . .
For a bunch of tulips, cheap, an armful for eighty cents! . . .
Home! A stairway up, or a driveway in over a hundred yards,
filled with the wreckage of woodchucks; or a tent
sagging from a downpour, wet ashes, food broken into
shells by a lousy raccoon with spectacular eyes and brows,
a black deep gaze like mine when I remember dinner in a hotel
with a view, a sea weighty with reflections and a hillside
of still bees!

Time was a scent in the woods.
Time was wind.
Time was a girl peeing, wiping with a kerchief and tossing it.
Time was urine, that we drank.
Time was a drink we bought, letting the glass slip while we kissed.
Time was a bit of shattered glass gone to sand.
Time was we were visible, with regrets, secrets, with intelligence,
that bolt from the blue.
Time was blue, we drank it.

For one late night, with the light low, the wax molten, the ink fast . . .
For one wet morning, the grass bitter, the sky shimmering like a lake.
For a lake, for a little algaed water.

What we could hold in our hands we crushed.
What we could carry we dropped.

I hear as I once heard mourning doves in my heating ducts,
knocking and roiling. Scratching metal like a windpipe.
What I wouldn't give for a little . . . And my flute, that I played
twenty years, that my lover gave me, memory. That cracked
song in it, that heartbeat when someone flies near me,
warping space. Darling,

do you hear me?
Time was consciousness of time.
Time was telling.
Time was our body,
full lower lip and teeth as straight as a wall,
a face as cut as a ridge,
planetary eyes, observatories to this constant season without
the lamp low, the stifling heat, the opportunity to love deeply
and completely your coming over, traveling earth as easily as
wings over the saguaro poles, pitted like craters.
Time was a date. Time was a magnification

of a cell that links and reproduces. What I wouldn't give
for a moment on a coastal train, adolescents hanging
from cramped passages, dirty sea air throwing sand,
and they wipe their faces with the backs of their dirty hands,
for that dirt, for two or three granules of smutty earth . . .

We were on that train, I can smell it now like the dead tuna
in the dead sea. We had eaten a greasy meal with mustard and
cumin seeds that runs down the wrist, soaks the bread, god
how the seeds stuck in my teeth, and the earth rocked and
the train stuttered and the world spun for a few more years.

Time was alchemy,
biting, combing, lifting you
from the birds of morning to night.
Now on a metaphoric level, on this
moon-from-behind, this celestial certainty —
clumps of igneous spewing like a furnace
for a face — I feel like a criminal with no
control, sleeping the sleep I have plundered into, I am lucky
to have done so. Time was energy, and now the earth is buried
in us, my nostalgia!

TUCSON MOON

It's where
we ended, intuiting the old
globe from afar,
darkened oceans, bald hills, bales of dried
witnesses, "children" playing
with a snake left for a belt in the desert,
and the hardening
artery "I love you" a torture
for the poor
melted earth, expected to yield a little shade,
a little harbor
that won't burn off when the sun cripples
the moonlit
morning, the Sonoran burning basin,
our carbonated brain
suturing its sky by writing to you now
of our nature
like a guided moon over a poster
planet, a blister
healing our first physical pleasure.

LUCKY PIERRE'S

Not a large meadow, not many lilies,
not completely cleared skies, a ladderless
moon, not, say, as final —
                               enchanted — or beautiful
as a curve in space, the whole environment

needing a little something, a limit
as once was said of people —

after a decent snack
of a vermilion poppy
from a hillside of thousands less one
state flower compensating
the tireless among us,

sightseers mount the foam
thinking more serious things,

"anyway there's nothing in this notebook,"
"lovemaking to the tune of x dollars, not love but a vacation,"

words someone will never forget on another planet
after this one is no more

a swatch of grass from which we imagine
a smokeless Golden Gate, rustproof bougainvillaea,
gods at their recital (some enchanted prom),
and only later the fog, only later the natural causes —

short-skirted waitresses smelling of eucalyptus,
a roving guitarist
as unexpected as another night.

COUNTRYSIDE

My darling works until she finishes   I resist starting —
    craning out the upper window over the tiled roofs
we each imagine the moon sets in night mist
    she says she sees it I pretend I don't

over our heads someone who makes a lot of money
    does something arty the public likes like pouring color
over red cherries —
    not delicious   wrong language

when she finally finishes I am in the kitchen again
    counting supplies wondering if we can return
neither thinks we've woken from a strange dream
    I'd gotten to the bottom of a sensation

tied up with doing nothing until I felt
    one way or the other   in other words nothing
and then being blown away by relationship never helps
    —did you do that?   No you made me —

it's all I can do to clean up from the night before
    light streaming off the ancient stones
small windows for defensive purposes   the whole village set on a slope
    the quest was for a form that wouldn't sacrifice presence

the answer Picasso is said to have given the German officer
    who asked   pointing to *Guernica*   did you do that? No you did that
it amounts to some ulcerated nights   some tangled hair
    beautiful old bottles   nets

songs before the sun is up
    not proscriptive but love all the same

such that I find I would never talk to anyone
        whose day doesn't last a month or a year

in town shopping we stop for soup
        the canopy's shoved back   there are stars for everyone
& get home drunk
        hoping the bread soaks the burn

mornings I read my tourist book
        ape the population rather than look American
when will I wise up?
        very warm & pleasant   birds despite the heat

we make love waiting to stop the spin by hand
        or the wash charges up again
someone drops by to see the kitchen made from the ruin
        this regular stuff emerges as an image

something scary something to hurt us
        to make us dead
& art —
        she never wakens me so when I'm awake I'm unguarded

could it be relationship & not matter with whom?
        as easily as this sky be a diagram & not an embrace
same sky different death's head behind it
        small jar of anchovies olive oil & salt

SONNET AGAINST NUCLEAR WEAPONS

The human sigh commuted to life imprisonment—
it's a sparrow in the hazels and pines.

A log, and so on and so forth,
anti-pastoral and realistic.

There was a dinner, you can see for yourself,
clean napkins, it might have been far worse,

entering a lit room undressed;
an unlit room, dressed.

It isn't anything you want to think about.
And went pale.

With a stranger for the first time in her life.
With a stranger for the first time in the afterlife.

The light in the room on both of them.
I'm writing on the back of a child's drawing,

a snake. Slightly protruding belly, creamy,
round breasts. Sometimes when I think of her

she remembers. Seven eyes of God
play the tape forward a little, stop it, replay it.

The phone's ringing in someone else's place.
—I'll get it.

When she thinks of moving tonight,
the seven eyes of god in the hazels and pines

enter an unlit room, a little
pale on the back of a child's drawing,

slightly protruding belly, and realistic.
It might have been far.

She remembers a human sigh against
the suppression of rights. A snake.

ART HISTORY

This hidden hag whose face belies the young face in front
                    is a shrine completely open
                                        so it's possible to observe
the image of the goddess from any angle, this new day

a face torn off; features now bunched together, scattered over
the battleground, a melancholy of alterations
                    for which language has only physical
                                                        analogies —

                                    her twist of mouth not so
dead that it cannot
(nothing spared) faceted, folded & twisted, hard like a wrench
not heal—

—We made it,
                                                hurtling
out of indulgence & not the other way around,
                                    tossed heads of gorged horses:

then we broke up;
                    the foreshortened depths
of the turns, & bit my nipple on the way out of her
life, the inside of a pleated bellow,
                    measured spans, slopes & hollows.

                    The gods had been busy on & off for days
when they asked a question of perspective as to whether
(strike the man entering the salon of a brothel with a faun, a chair, & a
                                                        bowl of fruit)
the beast in the lady is the back of her head
                    or her lover's hand.

                         It took everything to get her up in the morning
& out of the house
                    strewn urns, chairs, Japanese panels, & loosed
                                             over the goddamn
desert floor
                    (put x-rated after)
the recumbent sleeper with both arms overslung,
      the sleeper prone, belly to ground, cheek resting on arms,
a space filled with wonder, surety, desire, respect, daylight
& dark periods
                    such that everything exactly reversed
                                  is unbelievable & true,

the female nude's double pomes,
                    buttons & clefts, my darling,
mosquitoes on her, a harvest; a ruin.

TURNING OVER THE EARTH

Like beauty on a dark night there's more than you can see.
Earth moves less fast, the moon closer.
We come to capture it in our cages of white clothes.

Ferryman heaves off the cattails with no one visible
among the flooded rice plains of the Camargue.
Another memory: wild horses trampling the high grasses

beyond the mustard fields. Love goes to someone new
in a distant city, a divided city, a decent city.
The moon arrives shrouded like a bedroom

inland from the destruction —
mouths full of teeth collapsing,
cementing the surface and mounting sparkling white hotels.

After turning over the earth,
people in the country are eating quietly
in a place they fought for on the losing side,

doing the serviceable and natural thing,
the illegal thing of keeping the language alive.
Love must still be something

like rain that goes on after a storm.
Someone steps into the barn to be alone with her baby.
We wait to touch what seems a long time.

FOUNDERED STAR

Little fevered island, blued to closing,
boatmen, tidemen, shademen, men of color
and of peace;

women of the cabbage, women of the carrot-house,
women of the swim;
children squealing and picnicking, doe-eyed
and able-bodied, children of clashing cymbals and chalky
dreams, of milk-lips, of bugs under glass;

come now to the tips of the roofs, come now to the lake
lip, to the entryway of the tunnels, to the counting-house;

air the eiderdown, steam the rooms of the lovers, break
the fistfights from their arguments, marry the maid —

live a little in the afternoon, asking,
                         —now what do I do?

because this is the way we are alive, though we force ourselves out
of a certain nostalgia, where we first made love
the condition of our lives —
                         a dark room there, but only because
the shades were drawn, it was really midday!, and our clothes stuck
to our bodies like hairy beasts! — we watched the light change
in our eyes, as we dug deeper, pulling out embers —

remember? But the word itself is no longer magical,
the word no longer a living thing . . . a weakness in one of two breakers.

Yet there remains an image, when you water the sun and moon, mouths
coupling and uncoupling, kissing along the ridge the poet
invented, coincident, temporal, carnal, all

so that others might be entertained, changed a nick or two
like a diamond. Who can say whether better or worse, but this much
I can say, I who am always writing

                                        to you, my earthship, my
next life —
though no one is now
listening or talking (it's all the same)
though no one is now
laboring or sleeping (it's forbidden)
no one yet exploded, the globe forgives
the night sky gone yellow, the morning sea gone white
and all for a little greed, a little light on the wall,

a view of the other side — oar dipped in ink! —
where we shall never again believe things
about ourselves that aren't true.

THE ENCHANTED FOREST

That nothing intercept
the burning of our fates,
as sweet as an orchard

may we stand in the nude tiger-eyed
rather than be provided
an umbrella from the sun,

piercing the deaf-to-a-thousand-stories
the day after a war,
a cold-stopping chill

in the heart of a people.
Let us board up
like a hundred windows

giving onto hell
the material body of our message,
the joy in true contact

with things, merciful things,
the very bonds of an idiot society,
and stand on our last pivot,

a magnificent move, a steady, untoward
mountain of a move, and speak
in a straightforward manner

with the least important
least visited, raped, riddled
speech in nature,

no,
not from your balcony,
not outside your door

or within,
but to death's own
homesickness

speak with our eyes down on
the sex of our loved one
no one's name,

let no one out of clay and earth
grieve rain's rainbow,
love, alone,

yet say the face through the back of the head,
the front of a unicorn from behind,
horsing, shining — . . .

Jane Miller's awards include a Lila Wallace-Reader's Digest Writer's Award, Guggenheim and National Endowment for the Arts fellowships, a guest residency at The American Academy in Rome, the Four Corners Book Award, a Discovery Award, and a *Los Angeles Times* Book Award nomination. She won the National Poetry Series Open Competition in 1982 with *The Greater Leisures* and co-authored (with Olga Broumas) *Black Holes, Black Stockings*. Her collection of essays on poetry, culture, and travel, *Working Time,* was recently published by the University of Michigan Press. She has taught at Goddard College, The University of Iowa Writers' Workshop, and presently teaches at the University of Arizona in Tucson.